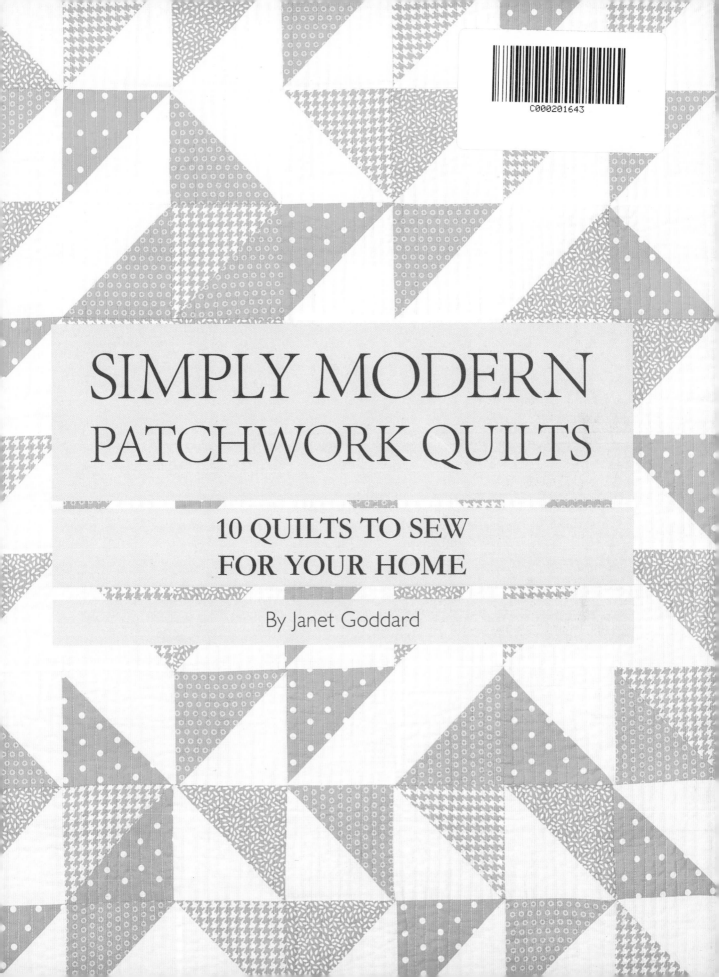

SIMPLY MODERN
PATCHWORK QUILTS

10 QUILTS TO SEW
FOR YOUR HOME

By Janet Goddard

Published in 2018 by
Search Press Ltd
Wellwood
North Farm Road
Tunbridge Wells
Kent, TN2 3DR
UK

ISBN: 978-1-78221-598-1

Conceived, designed and produced by
Quail Publishing
The Incuba, 1 Brewers Hill Road,
Dunstable,
Bedfordshire,
LU6 1AA

Creative Director: Darren Brant
Art Editor: Georgina Brant
Graphic Design: Quail Studio
Editor: Elizabeth Betts
Photography: Jarek Duk
Fabric Support: Mez Crafts, Makower,
The Cotton Patch

Printed in China

CONTENTS

Introduction   6

Measurements   7

Fabric and Thread   7

Equipment   8

PROJECTS   **21**

Falling Arrows   22

Floating Triangles   28

Hugs and Kisses   34

Triangle Jumble   40

Soundwaves   46

Springtime Maze   52

Squares in the Corner   58

Starbust   66

Stepping Stones   72

Scrap Happy   78

TECHNIQUES   **85**

Rotary Cutting   86

Patchwork Techniques   88

Quilting   92

Introduction

Simply Modern Patchwork Quilts are fresh, bright and modern. Here you will find ten different patterns, featuring a variety of designs, to create your own stylish quilts.

I have used brightly patterned fabrics, combined with simple plains, to make my quilts. The combination of the two showcases the geometric shapes created by the patchwork. To speed up, and therefore simplify the process, there are no pattern pieces as all you need is a rotary cutting set. Each quilt pattern includes sewing instructions, step-by-step photos, information for quilting and handy hints.

Sections on patchwork and quilting techniques can be found at the back of the book (page 85) and I suggest that you read these first before beginning. These provide a really good starting point and describe all the basics in detail.

The projects are designed to be completed in a weekend or a couple of weeks so are easily achievable and are graded as 'Easy' or 'Requires Experience'. Basic sewing skills are needed for the 'Easy' projects and are suitable for beginners. The 'Requires Experience' projects have more steps and will take a little longer to make. Just remember to read the Patchwork Techniques section before starting.

Each of the quilt projects could easily be made smaller or larger. To do this, either increase or decrease the number of blocks in the quilt and adjust the fabric quantities as required. The quilts are all quilted on a domestic sewing machine with simple straight line or wavy quilting.

A patchwork quilt made with love is a happy quilt for both the maker and the recipient, so I hope that you love making the quilts in this book.

Janet Goddard

MEASUREMENTS

All the cutting instructions for these projects include a 0.65cm (¼in) seam allowance. I have used metric as the standard measurement throughout all my patterns but the imperial measurements have been included as well. Please use either centimetres or inches but do not mix the two together.

FABRIC AND THREAD

One of the nicest parts of starting a new project is being able to choose the fabrics. I have made fabric choices to suit the quilt design. If the patchwork uses large shapes I have tended to use fabric that has a larger scale print design; for smaller shapes the fabric print has tended to be smaller as well.

All of the quilts in this book use fabric that is 100 per cent cotton and of a high-quality. If different fabric weights are used together it can adversely affect the overall quality and strength of the finished quilt. Quilts used for day-to-day use need to be hard-wearing and if you skimp on the quality of the fabric the quilts will not last.

The fabrics used for the quilts in this book are bright, modern and there are a variety of patterns. Each project details the fabric colour and print used but you can substitute your own fabric choices to suit.

The fabric allowances in the patterns are for fabric that is approximately 107cm (42in) wide from selvedge to selvedge. I always cut the

selvedge from the fabric before beginning a project and rarely pre-wash fabrics, but this is a personal choice.

The fabric allowances in each pattern allow for approximately 5–7.5cm (2–3in) extra, so if a small mistake is made you shouldn't run out of fabric. However, that being said, do try to be as careful as possible.

The best thread for patchwork is high quality cotton thread. I tend to use a 50-weight grey thread for all the piecing. For quilting I use a 40-weight thread in a colour that complements or contrasts with the fabric.

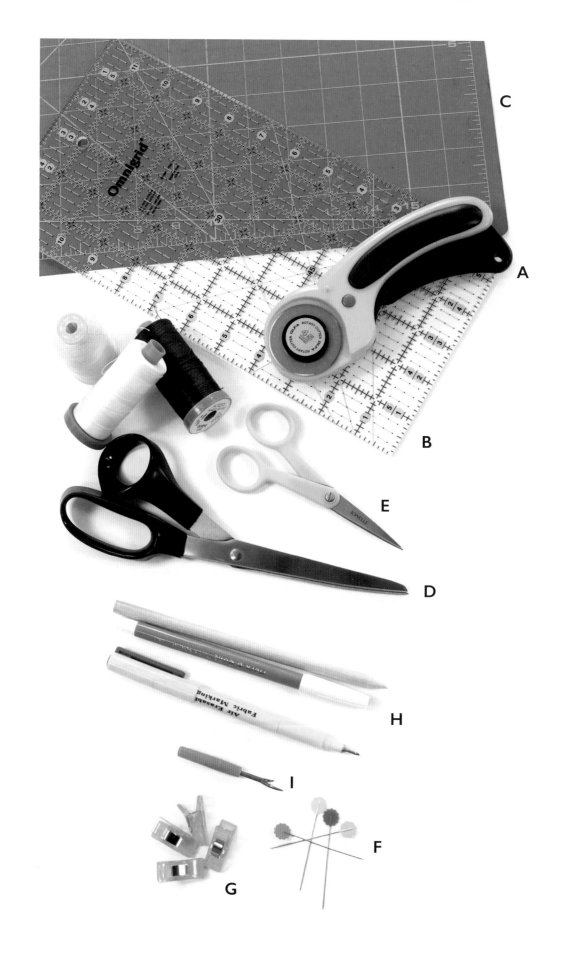

A

B

C

D

E

F

G

H

I

EQUIPMENT

Good quality basic equipment is needed. There is no need to spend a fortune on the latest gadgets, just invest in some good quality essential resources.

Sewing machine: The most important piece of equipment for patchwork and quilting is a sewing machine. It really only needs to be able to stitch forwards and backwards and doesn't need a whole lot of fancy stitches. It is important that your machine is cared for and is cleaned and serviced regularly to keep it working well. A little oil applied, according to the manufacturer's instructions, should help to keep everything in good order. Changing the needle regularly also helps with the quality of stitching, and I usually change the needle on the machine every time I begin a new project. The two machine feet used the most are the 0.65cm (¼in) patchwork foot which is excellent for maintaining 0.65cm (¼in) wide seams, and the walking foot used for machine quilting.

Rotary cutter, ruler and mat: All the pieces for the quilt projects in this book can be cut using a rotary cutter (**A**), ruler (**B**) and a rotary cutting mat (**C**). A rotary cutter is a cutting instrument with a round-wheeled blade. This is used with an acrylic ruler and a self-healing cutting mat.

A good quality rotary cutter should have a protective safety shield on it that can be pushed on and off. It is important to train yourself to always make sure that the safety cover is on the blade every time the cutter is put down. Blades are sharp and can cut through up to eight layers of fabric at a time, and so can do a lot of damage to hands if not kept safe. Replace the blades when they start to become blunt.

Rulers come in many shapes and sizes, are marked in centimetres or inches and are made of tough acrylic. I personally find the rulers with yellow markings the easiest to see on fabric but this is a personal choice. If you are purchasing just one ruler make it a 15 x 61cm (6 x 24in) ruler as this can be used for most projects.

A rotary cutting mat is a self-healing mat designed to be used with a rotary cutter. Mats come with grid markings on them which can be used with the ruler for accurate cutting. If you are purchasing a mat for the first time buy the largest you can afford. A 61 x 91cm (24 x 36in) mat is a good investment.

Scissors: A good sharp pair of dress-making scissors (**D**) is essential for tasks such as cutting through cotton wadding. A small pair (**E**) is also handy for snipping threads.

Pins: I use flat flowerhead fine pins (**F**) for patchwork as they help to keep the fabric flat, but any type of pins will do.

Needles: Hand sewing needles are used for some finishing off techniques and are available in many sizes. Sharps are good for general sewing and hand stitching binding.

Clips: (**G**)These are a recent addition to the sewing world and are great for holding multiple layers together when hand stitching a binding to a quilt. The clips are plastic (think mini clothes pegs but better) and can be removed easily as you stitch.

Fabric markers: There are many fabric markers (**H**) available but any marker should be easy to use, easy to see and simple to remove after you have finished sewing. Markers are used to mark measurements for cutting or stitching and also quilting lines or patterns. Several different markers are needed in order to contrast with both light and dark fabrics. White and silver markers, water-erasable pens and charcoal markers are all useful.

Seam ripper: (**I**)This is often called a 'quick unpick' and usually comes as a tool with the sewing machine. Hugely useful for removing tacking (basting) stitches or the odd mistake we all make now and then.

Iron and ironing board: After the sewing machine the iron is the most useful tool quilt making. A press with a dry iron is all that is needed and the use of a good quality iron does make a difference to the finished product. The ironing surface needs to be firm and clean.

Projects

10 modern patchwork quilt designs.

Falling Arrows
page 22

Floating Triangles
page 28

Hugs and Kisses
page 34

Triangle Jumble
page 40

Soundwaves

page 46

Springtime Maze
page 52

Squares in the Corner
page 58

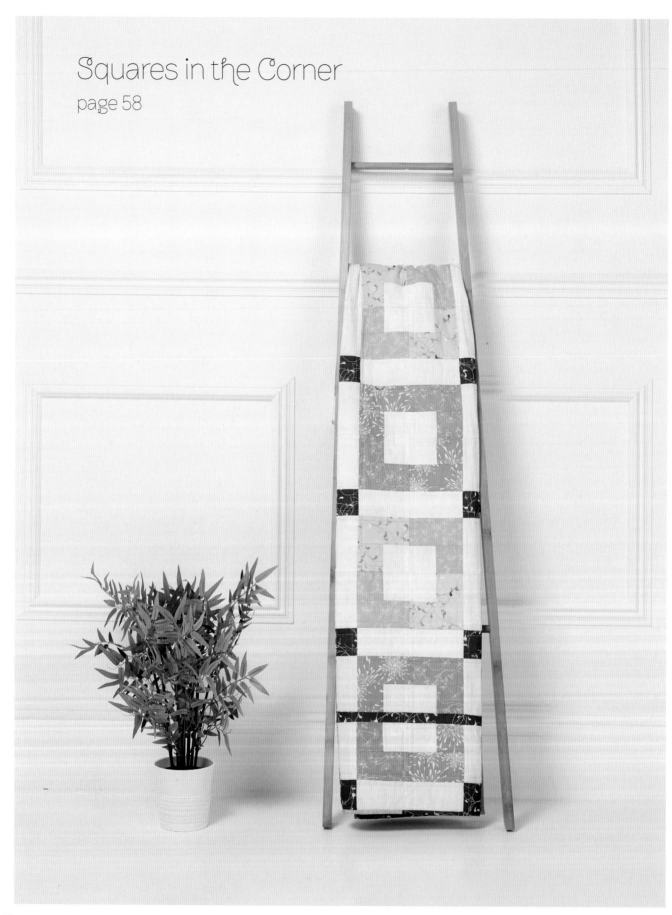

Starburst

page 66

Stepping Stones
page 72

Scrap Happy
page 78

Falling Arrows

This speedy project is a perfect make if you are short on time.

This speedy project is a perfect make if you are short on time.

Size: 123 x 161.5cm (48½ x 63½in)

SKILL LEVEL: EASY

The bold blocks in this quilt help to make this a quick project to stitch. The method used to construct the triangle units is a fast technique with very little fabric wastage. That is always a bonus in my book!

PREPARATION

The quilt centre is made up of five columns of arrows, each one made of nine arrows and one background filler block. There are two columns of arrows from each patterned fabric and one column of blue arrows. Each arrow block, in the finished quilt, measures 15.25cm (6in) square.

MATERIALS

FABRIC
Requirements based on fabrics with a useable width of 107cm (42in):
- 3m (120in) light fabric for the background and borders
- 75cm (30in) blue patterned fabric for the arrows and binding
- 50cm (20in) patterned fabric one for the arrows
- 50cm (20in) patterned fabric two for the arrows
- 132 x 157.5cm (52 x 62in) light fabric for the backing

WADDING (BATTING)
- 132 x 157.5cm (52 x 62in)

HABERDASHERY
- Neutral thread for piecing
- Beige thread for quilting

CUTTING

All cutting instructions include a 0.65cm (¼in) seam allowance.

Background fabric

- Six 8.9 x 146cm (3½ x 57½in) strips from the length of the fabric for the inner and outer borders
- Two 8.9 x 123cm (3½ x 48½in) strips from the length of the fabric for the top and bottom borders (join to get the required length)
- Thirteen 18.4cm (7¼in) squares
- Fifty-two 9.8cm (3⅞in) squares
- Five 8.9 x 16.5cm (3½ x 6½in) rectangles

Blue fabric

- Three 18.4cm (7¼in) squares
- Twelve 9.8cm (3⅞in) squares
- Six 5cm (2in) x WOF strips for the binding

Patterned fabric one

- Five 18.4cm (7¼in) squares
- Twenty 9.8cm (3⅞in) squares

Patterned fabric two

- Five 18.4cm (7¼in) squares
- Twenty 9.8cm (3⅞in) squares

STEP BY STEP

TO STITCH ARROW BLOCKS FROM THE BLUE FABRIC:

1. Draw a line on the diagonal from corner to corner on the wrong side of twelve 9.8cm (3⅞in) background fabric squares.

2. Take one 18.4cm (7¼in) blue square and two 9.8cm (3⅞in) background fabric squares. Place the background squares on top of the blue square, right sides together, on diagonally opposite corners. Pin, then stitch a scant 0.65cm (¼in) away from each side of the drawn line. **(A)**

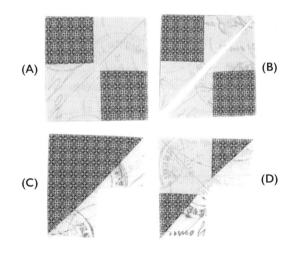

(A) (B)

(C) (D)

3. Cut along the drawn line to make two units **(B)**. Press seams towards the small triangles **(C)**.

4. Position another two 9.8cm (3⅞in) background squares on the remaining unsewn corner of each unit so that the diagonal line is positioned between the two smaller triangles. Stitch a scant 0.65cm (¼in) away from each side of the drawn line **(D)**.

5. Cut along the drawn line **(E)**. Press seams towards the small triangles and trim points.

6. Repeat steps 2 to 5 to make a total of twelve upper units **(F)**.

7. To make the lower units, take three 18.4cm (7¼in) background squares and twelve 9.8cm (3⅞in) blue squares and repeat steps 1 to 6. The fabrics in these units will be in the opposite order to those stitched earlier.

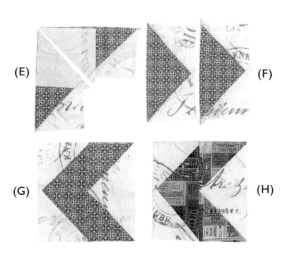

(E)   (F)

(G)   (H)

8. Stitch each upper unit to the top of a lower unit to make an arrow design. Press seams towards the large background triangle **(G)**.

9. Stitch the units into a column of nine arrows; there will be three arrow units left over and not needed for this quilt. Counting down from the top, between units six and seven, stitch a 8.9 x 16.5cm (3½ x 6½in) background rectangle. Press all seams downwards.

TO STITCH ARROW BLOCKS FROM PATTERNED FABRIC ONE:

10. Repeat steps 1 to 9 with patterned fabric one to create a total of twenty arrow designs **(H)**. There will be two arrow blocks left over and not needed for this quilt. When stitching the arrows together into two columns, stitch the background rectangles between units four and five.

TO STITCH ARROW BLOCKS FROM PATTERNED FABRIC TWO:

11. Repeat steps 1 to 9 with patterned fabric two to create a total of twenty lower and upper units. There will be two arrow blocks left over and not needed for this quilt. When stitching the arrows together into two columns, stitch the background rectangles between units seven and eight.

TO STITCH THE COLUMNS TOGETHER AND ADD THE BORDERS:

12. Stitch the columns together, adding an 8.9 x 146cm (3½ x 57½in) strip of background fabric between each column and on both sides of the quilt. Press seams towards the background strips.

13. Stitch an 8.9 x 123cm (3½ x 48½in) strip of background fabric to the top and bottom of the quilt. Press seams towards the background strips.

TO FINISH THE QUILT:

14. Layer the quilt top by placing the backing fabric wrong side up onto a clean surface, followed by the wadding (batting) and then the quilt top, centrally placed and right side up. The backing and wadding (batting) are slightly larger than the quilt top. Secure the quilt sandwich by tacking (basting) or with quilters' pins placed at regular intervals.

15. The quilt is machine quilted with a beige thread in vertical lines, stitching through the centre of each arrow and then 1.3cm (½in) in from each seam line. Start the first line of quilting in the centre of the quilt and work outwards towards each edge.

16. To bind the quilt, trim the excess backing and wadding (batting) level with the quilt top edges. Stitch the blue binding strips together to form one continuous strip. Press seams open to reduce bulk. Fold the strip in half lengthwise, wrong sides together, and press. Match the raw edges of the binding to the raw edges of the quilt and sew in place. Fold the binding over to the back of the quilt and neatly slip stitch in place by hand.

Floating Triangles

Colourful triangles float across this graphic quilt.

Colourful triangles float across this graphic quilt.

Size: 103 x 131cm (40½ x 51½in)

SKILL LEVEL: EASY

The mid grey background fabric really sets off the colourful triangles which appear to float across the quilt. The wonderful thing about this project is that it is super quick to make, with each triangle unit having just four pieces. A great finish in a weekend project.

PREPARATION

The quilt centre is made up of forty-eight blocks. Each block, in the finished quilt, measures 14cm (5½in) square. This design is not suitable for fabrics with a one-way pattern.

MATERIALS

FABRIC
Requirements based on fabrics with a useable width of 107cm (42in):
- 1.75m (70in) grey fabric for the background and outer border
- 15.25cm (6in) pink fabric for the triangles
- 15.25cm (6in) blue fabric for the triangles
- 15.25cm (6in) green fabric for the triangles
- 15.25cm (6in) yellow fabric for the triangles
- 15.25cm (6in) cream fabric for the triangles
- 40.6cm (16in) orange fabric for the triangles and binding

- 112 x 140m (44 x 55in) pink fabric for the backing

WADDING (BATTING)
- 112 x 140m (44 x 55in)

HABERDASHERY
- Neutral thread for piecing
- Dark grey thread for quilting

CUTTING

All cutting instructions include a 0.65cm (¼in) seam allowance.

Grey fabric
- Twenty-four 12.4cm (4⅞in) squares
- Forty-eight 5 x 11.5cm (2 x 4½in) strips
- Forty-eight 5 x 15.25cm (2 x 6in) strips
- Two 10 x 103cm (4 x 40½in) strips for the border
- Two 10 x 112cm (4 x 44in) strips for the border (join to get the required length)

Blue, pink, green, yellow, cream fabrics
- Four 12.4cm (4⅞in) squares

Orange fabric
- Four 12.4cm (4⅞in) squares
- Five 5cm (2in) x WOF strips for the binding

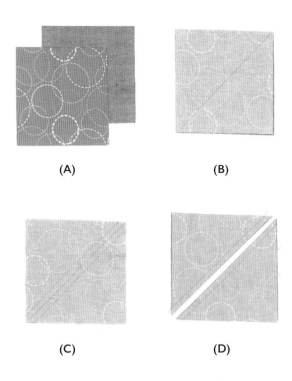

(A)　　　　　　　　(B)

(C)　　　　　　　　(D)

3. Cut along the drawn line **(D)**, and press seams towards the grey fabric **(E)**. Trim points. This yields two half-square triangle units.

STEP BY STEP

TO STITCH THE BLOCKS:

1. Take one 12.4cm (4⅞in) grey square and one 12.4cm (4⅞in) pink square **(A)**. Draw a line on the diagonal from corner to corner on the wrong side of the pink square **(B)**.

2. Place the squares right sides together and stitch a scant 0.65cm (¼in) away from each side of the drawn line **(C)**.

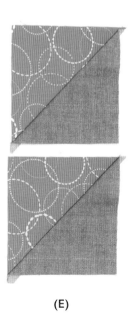

(E)

4. Stitch a 5 × 11.5cm (2 × 4½in) grey strip to the side of one of the units completed in step 3 **(F)**. It is important that the grey strip is stitched to the side with the pink triangle. Press seam towards the grey fabric.

5. Stitch a 5cm × 15.25cm (2 × 6in) grey strip to the remaining pink side of the unit stitched in step 4 **(G)**. Press seam towards the grey fabric.

6. Continue in this way, using all the 12.4cm (4⅞in) grey and coloured squares until forty-eight blocks are stitched.

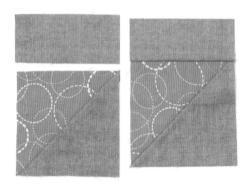

(F)

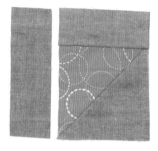

(G)

TO STITCH THE BLOCKS TOGETHER:

7. Lay out the blocks in a grid design six across and eight down. Each horizontal row has one block of each colour and the coloured blocks move across in each row to create the diagonal coloured pattern. Rotate every second block to create the floating effect.

8. Sew the blocks into eight rows of six blocks. Press the seams in each row in opposite directions.

9. Stitch the rows together. Press all seams downwards.

TO STITCH THE OUTER BORDER:

10. Stitch a 10 × 112cm (4 × 44in) grey strip to opposite sides of the quilt. Press seams towards the border.

11. Stitch a 10 × 103cm (4 × 40½in) grey strip to the top and bottom of the quilt. Press seams towards the border.

TO FINISH THE QUILT:

12. Layer the quilt top by placing the backing fabric wrong side up on a clean surface, followed by the wadding (batting) and then the quilt top, centrally placed and right side up. The backing and wadding (batting) are slightly larger than the quilt top. Secure the quilt sandwich by tacking (basting) or with quilters' pins placed at regular intervals.

13. The quilt is machine quilted with a dark grey thread in diagonal lines through the centre of the triangles on every second row.

14. To bind the quilt, trim the excess backing and wadding (batting) level with the quilt top edges. Stitch the orange binding strips together to form one continuous strip. Press seams open to reduce bulk. Fold the strip in half lengthwise, wrong sides together, and press. Match the raw edges of the binding to the raw edges of the quilt and sew in place. Fold the binding over to the back of the quilt and neatly slip stitch in place by hand.

HANDY HINTS:

• It is very important that when stitching the 5 × 11.5cm (2 × 4½in) and 5 × 15.25cm (2 × 6in) grey strips to the triangle units that they are stitched to the same side for every block. Once you have made one block, put it next to the machine and use it as a reference point while making the others.

• This quilt has been quilted in a very minimalistic way so as not to distract from the design of the quilt. The quilting took just 75 minutes from start to finish, so really is quick to do.

Hugs and Kisses

This vibrant quilt is perfect for a loved one.

This vibrant quilt is perfect for a loved one.

Size: 131 x 159.4cm (51½ x 62¾in)

SKILL LEVEL: REQUIRES EXPERIENCE

There are so many different patterns in this quilt, from intersecting floral lines to bright jade green crosses, yet it is made from just one repeating block. The combination of print and plain fabrics help create the visual effect.

PREPARATION
The quilt is made up of twenty blocks. Each block, in the finished quilt, measures 28.6cm (11¼in) square.

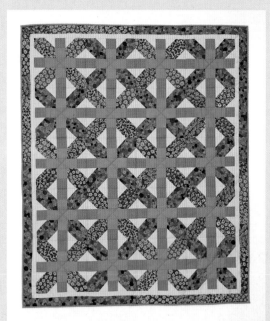

MATERIALS

FABRIC
Requirements based on fabrics with a useable width of 107cm (42in):
- 1.25m (50in) plain lilac fabric for the background and inner border
- 1m (40in) patterned fabric one for the patchwork and outer border
- 1m (40in) patterned fabric two for the patchwork and outer border
- 1m (40in) plain jade fabric for the patchwork and binding
- 63.5cm (25in) plain purple fabric for the patchwork
- 142 x 170cm (56 x 67in) blue patterned fabric for the backing

WADDING (BATTING)
- 142 x 170cm (56 x 67in)

HABERDASHERY
- Neutral thread for piecing
- Grey thread for quilting

CUTTING

All cutting instructions include a 0.65cm (¼in) seam allowance.

Lilac fabric
- One hundred and sixty 7cm (2¾in) squares
- Two 4 × 144cm (1½ × 56¾in) strips for the inner border (join to get the required length)
- Two 4 × 120.8cm (1½ × 47½in) strips for the inner border (join to get the required length)

Patterned fabric one
- Forty 12.7cm (5in) squares
- Two 6.3 × 75.2cm (2½ × 29⅝in) strips for the outer border
- Two 6.3 × 66cm (2½ × 26in) strips for the outer border

Patterned fabric two
- Forty 12.7cm (5in) squares
- Two 6.3 × 74.6cm (2½ × 29⅜in) strips for the outer border
- Two 6.3 × 66cm (2½ × 26in) strips for the outer border

Jade fabric
- Forty 7cm (2¾in) squares
- Twenty 7 × 18.4cm (2¾ × 7¼in) rectangles
- Five 5cm (2in) × WOF strips for the binding

Purple fabric
- Eighty 7cm (2¾in) squares

STEP BY STEP

TO STITCH THE BLOCKS:

1. Take eight 7cm (2¾in) lilac squares and draw a line on the diagonal from corner to corner on the wrong side of each square.

2. Take four 12.7cm (5in) patterned fabric one squares and on each one place two lilac squares from step 1 on diagonally opposite corners **(A)**. Stitch along the drawn lines. Trim seams and flip back each triangle **(B)**. Press seams towards the triangle.

3. Take two 7cm (2¾in) jade squares and two 7cm (2¾in) purple squares and stitch together in pairs. Press seams towards the jade squares **(C)**.

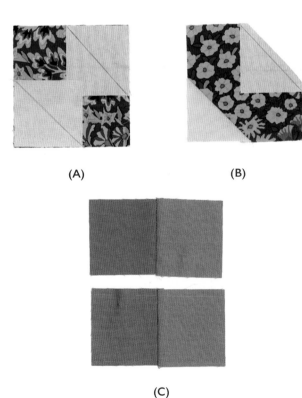

(A) (B)

(C)

4. Take one 7 × 18.4cm (2¾ × 7¼in) jade rectangle and stitch a 7cm (2¾in) purple square to each end of the rectangle **(D)**. Press seams towards the rectangle.

5. Stitch the units completed in step 2 to each side of a unit completed in step 3 **(E)**. Ensure that the units are correctly positioned before sewing. Press seams away from the centre.

6. Stitch the units from step 5 to each side of the unit from step 4 and press seams towards the rectangle **(F)**. Your block will measure 31.5cm (11¾in) square.

7. Repeat steps 1 to 6 to make a total of ten blocks.

8. Repeat steps 1 to 7 to make a further ten blocks, but substitute patterned fabric one for patterned fabric two. When pressing the seams of these blocks in step 5 press the seams towards the centre, and in step 6 press the seams away from the rectangle unit. This will ensure that the seams nest together when the blocks are joined.

TO STITCH THE BLOCKS TOGETHER:

9. Lay out the twenty blocks in a grid design four across and five down, alternating the blocks between patterned fabric one and two.

10. Sew the blocks into five rows of four blocks. Press the seams in each row in opposite directions.

11. Stitch the rows together. Press all seams downwards.

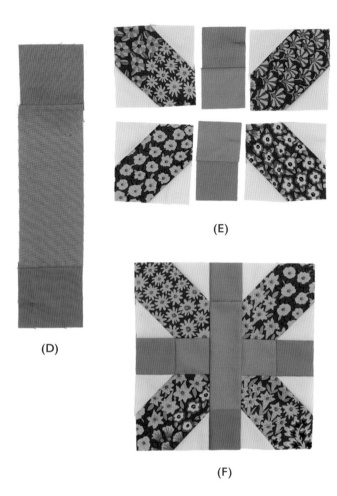

(D)

(E)

(F)

TO STITCH THE INNER AND OUTER BORDERS:

12. Stitch a 4 × 144cm (1½ × 56¾in) lilac inner border strip to opposite sides of the quilt. Press seams towards the border.

13. Stitch a 4 × 120.8cm (1½ × 47½in) lilac inner border strip to the top and bottom of the quilt. Press seams towards the border.

14. To stitch the outer border sew each 6.3 × 74.6cm (2½ × 29⅝in) patterned fabric one strip to a 6.3 × 75.6cm

(2½ × 29⅝in) patterned fabric two strip. Press seams open. Stitch to each side of the quilt top, reversing the strips so that fabric one and two are opposite to each other in the borders. Press seams away from the quilt centre.

15. Stitch each 6.3 × 66cm (2½ × 26in) patterned fabric one strip to a 6.3 × 66cm (2½ × 26in) patterned fabric two strip. Press seams open. Stitch to the top and bottom of the quilt so that the fabrics match at the corners.

TO FINISH THE QUILT:

16. Layer the quilt top by placing the backing fabric wrong side up on a clean surface, followed by the wadding (batting) and then the quilt top, centrally placed and right side up. The backing and wadding (batting) are slightly larger than the quilt top. Secure the quilt sandwich by tacking (basting) or with quilters' pins placed at regular intervals.

17. The quilt is machine quilted with grey thread in diagonal lines through the centre of each block. It is then quilted in the ditch

between the blocks, both horizontally and vertically.

18. To bind the quilt, trim the excess backing and wadding so that they are level with the quilt top edges. Stitch the jade binding strips together to form one continuous strip. Press seams open to reduce bulk. Fold the strip in half lengthwise, wrong sides together, and press. Match the raw edges of the binding to the raw edges of the quilt and sew in place. Fold the binding over to the back of the quilt and neatly slip stitch in place by hand.

HANDY HINTS:

• Quilting in the ditch is a very effective way of quilting where you do not have to worry if your stitching is straight, because they sit the seam line. This creates a quilted effect without seeing the actual stitches.

• There are quite a lot of seams to match up in this quilt, but if you press the seams as indicated in the instructions they will nest together and match perfectly.

• Save the small triangles cut off from the corners of the units pieced in step 2 and use them to make little pin cushions or mini patchwork.

Triangle Jumble

Which way will your triangles go?

Which way will your triangles go?

Size: 154 x 204cm (60½ x 80½in)

SKILL LEVEL: EASY

This is a simple, but spectacular quilt, that showcases triangles going every which way. The fun thing about this quilt is that once you have made all the triangle units you can be as creative as you like by mixing them up to create secondary patterns.

PREPARATION
The quilt is made up of one hundred and forty half-square triangle units. Each one, in the finished quilt, measures 12.7cm (5in) square.

MATERIALS

FABRIC
Requirements based on fabrics with a useable width of 107cm (42in):
- 2m (80in) white fabric for the background and inner border
- 75cm (30in) each of four yellow fabrics for the triangles
- 1.25m (50in) yellow spot fabric for the outer border and binding
- 165 x 216 cm (65 x 85in) yellow fabric for the backing

WADDING (BATTING)
- 165 x 216cm (65 x 85in) wadding

HABERDASHERY
- Neutral thread for piecing
- Pale yellow thread for quilting

CUTTING

All cutting instructions include a 0.65cm (¼ in) seam allowance.

White fabric

- Sixty-seven 14.9cm (5⅞ in) squares, each cross cut once on the diagonal to yield one hundred and thirty-four half-square triangles
- Two 5 × 179cm (2 × 70½ in) strips for the inner border (join to get the required length)
- Two 5 × 136cm (2 × 53½ in) strips for the inner border (join to get the required length)

Yellow fabrics

- Eighteen 14.9cm (5⅞ in) squares from each of three of the yellow fabrics, each cross cut once on the diagonal to yield thirty-six half-square triangles from each fabric
- Nineteen 14.9cm (5⅞ in) squares from one yellow fabric, each cross cut once on the diagonal to yield thirty-eight half-square triangles
- In total, there should be one hundred and forty-six yellow triangles

Yellow spot fabric

- Two 10 × 186cm (4 × 73½ in) strips for the outer border (join to get the required length)
- Two 10 × 154cm (4 × 60½ in) strips for the outer border (join to get the required length)
- Eight 5cm (2in) × WOF strips for the binding

STEP BY STEP

TO STITCH THE TRIANGLE UNITS:

1. Take twelve mixed fabric yellow triangles and place them together in pairs, right sides facing. Stitch together along the diagonal line. Press seams towards the darker fabric and trim points. This will yield six completed units **(A)**.

2. Take the remaining one hundred and thirty-four yellow triangles and stitch each to a white triangle, stitching along the diagonal line. Press seams towards the yellow fabric and trim points **(B)**.

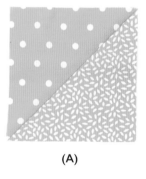

(A)

(B)

TO STITCH THE UNITS TOGETHER:

3. Lay out the one hundred and forty triangle units in a grid design, ten across and fourteen down. Turn the units around to create secondary patterns with the triangles. You will find that you can make all kinds of shapes including stars, squares, ticks and diagonal patterns.

4. Once you are happy with the quilt layout stitch the blocks in the horizontal rows together. Press the seams in each row in opposite directions.

5. Stitch the rows together. Press all seams downwards.

TO STITCH THE INNER AND OUTER BORDERS:

6. Stitch a 5 × 179cm (2 × 70½in) white border strip to opposite sides of the quilt. Press seams towards the border.

7. Stitch a 5 × 136cm (2 × 53½in) white border strip to the top and bottom of the quilt. Press seams towards the border.

8. Stitch a 10 × 186cm (4 × 73½in) yellow spot border strip to opposite sides of the quilt. Press seams towards the border.

9. Stitch a 10 × 154cm (4 × 60½in) yellow spot border strip to the top and bottom of the quilt. Press seams towards the border.

TO FINISH THE QUILT:

10. Layer the quilt top by placing the backing fabric wrong side up on a clean surface, followed by the wadding (batting) and then the quilt top, centrally placed and right side up. The backing and wadding (batting) are slightly larger than the quilt top. Secure the quilt sandwich by tacking (basting) or with quilters' pins placed at regular intervals.

11. The quilt is machine quilted with pale yellow thread in vertical lines 1.3cm (½in) apart. Start the first line of quilting in the centre of the quilt by using the vertical centre seam line as a guide. After this use the width of the walking foot as a guide.

12. To bind the quilt, trim the excess backing and wadding (batting) level with the quilt top edges. Stitch the yellow spot binding strips together to form one continuous strip. Press seams open to reduce bulk. Fold the strip in half lengthwise, wrong sides together, and press. Match the raw edges of the binding to the raw edges of the quilt and sew in place. Fold the binding over to the back of the quilt and neatly slip stitch in place by hand.

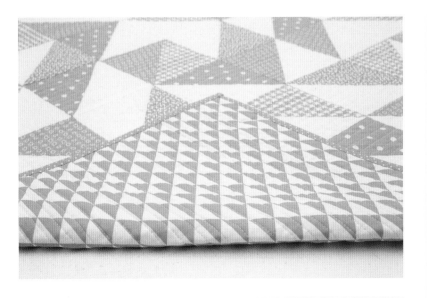

HANDY HINTS:

• The diagonal edges of the triangles are cut on the bias, so when you are stitching the units together be very careful not to stretch the fabric.

• When constructing the triangle units it is a good idea to chain piece them in batches of twenty units at a time. This saves time cutting the threads and stopping and starting the stitching. To chain piece, stitch to almost the end of a unit then position the next unit to be stitched under the machine foot, with just a small gap in between. Continue stitching. The units will be linked together by thread which can be cut apart when all the units have been stitched.

• When you have laid out all the units and are happy with the secondary patterns that you have created, label each row with a number so that they don't become muddled up when sewing.

Soundwaves

Stitch a rainbow of digital sound waves.

Stitch a rainbow of digital sound waves.

Size: 133 x 149cm (52½ x 58½in)

SKILL LEVEL: EASY

Fabric strips in graded colours move up and down like sound waves across the quilt. This is an excellent project for using up pre-cut 6.3cm (2½in) strips, and you can have great fun grading the fabric colours into a pleasing design.

PREPARATION

The quilt is made up of three rows, each showcasing a different colour wave. Each row is made up of a repeating pattern of three units, each of which contains one fabric strip from the colour family.

MATERIALS

FABRIC
Requirements based on fabrics with a useable width of 107cm (42in):
- 2m (80in) plain grey fabric for the background, borders and binding
- Eight 6.4cm (2½in) strips of yellow and green fabrics for the sound waves
- Eight 6.4cm (2½in) strips of orange and pink fabrics for the sound waves
- Eight 6.4cm (2½in) strips of purple, teal and blue fabrics for the sound waves

- 142 x 157.5cm (56 x 62in) grey patterned fabric for the backing

WADDING (BATTING)
- 142 x 157.5cm (56 x 62in)

HABERDASHERY
- Neutral thread for piecing
- Dark grey thread for quilting

CUTTING

All cutting instructions include a 0.65cm (¼ in) seam allowance.

Grey fabric

- Two 6.3 × 123cm (2½ × 48½in) strips for the outer border (join to get the required length)
- Two 14 × 133cm (5½ × 52½in) strips for the outer border (join to get the required length)
- Six 5cm (2in) × WOF strips for the binding
- Eighteen 6.4 × 21.6cm (2½ × 8½in) strips
- Thirty-six 6.4 × 16.5cm (2½ × 6½in) strips
- Thirty-six 6.4 × 11.5cm (2½ × 4½in) strips
- Thirty-six 6.4cm (2½in) squares

Yellow/green fabrics

- Three 6.3 × 21.6cm (2½ × 8½in) strips from each fabric

Orange/pink fabrics

- Three 6.3 × 21.6cm (2½ × 8½in) strips from each fabric

Purple/teal/blue fabrics

- Three 6.3 × 21.6cm (2½ × 8½in) strips from each fabric

STEP BY STEP

TO STITCH THE YELLOW/ GREEN ROW:

1. Take one of each of the yellow/green fabric strips and arrange them in a pleasing order, ensuring that the colours are graded and that fabrics are mixed up.

2. Using the first eight yellow/green strips, stitch the short ends of the fabric strips together in the following order:
- Strip one 21.6cm (8½in) grey to a 21.6cm (8½in) colour
- Strip two 16.5cm (6½in) grey to a 21.6cm (8½in) colour to a 6.4cm (2½in) grey
- Strip three 11.5cm (4½in) grey to a 21.6cm (8½in) colour to a 11.5cm (4½in) grey
- Strip four 6.4cm (2½in) grey to a 21.6cm (8½in) colour to a 16.5cm (6½in) grey
- Strip five 21.6cm (8½in) colour to a 21.6cm (8½in) grey
- Strip six 6.4cm (2½in) grey to a 21.6cm (8½in) colour to a 16.5cm (6½in) grey
- Strip seven 11.5cm (4½in) grey to a 21.6cm (8½in) colour to a 11.5cm (4½in) grey
- Strip eight 16.5cm (6½in) grey to a 21.6cm (8½in) colour to a 6.3cm (2½in) grey

3. Press seams towards the grey fabric **(A)**. Strips should measure 42cm (16½in) long **(B)**.

(A)

4. Stitch the eight strips together being careful not to mix up the order **(C)**. Press all seams towards the left **(D)**.

5. Repeat steps 2 to 4 with the remaining two sets of yellow/green strips, ensuring that the fabric placement is identical to the first unit.

6. Stitch the three units together to make the first row.

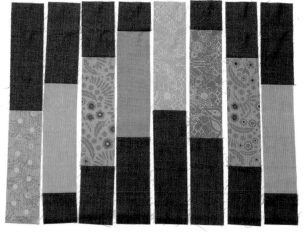

(B)

TO STITCH THE ORANGE/ PINK ROW:
7. Repeat as for the yellow/green row but press all seams towards the right.

TO STITCH THE PURPLE/TEAL/ BLUE ROW:
8. Repeat as for the yellow/green row, but press all seams towards the left.

(C)

TO STITCH THE ROWS TOGETHER:
9. Sew the three rows together, carefully matching the seams.

TO STITCH THE OUTER BORDER:
10. Stitch a 6.4 x 123cm (2½ x 48½in) grey strip to opposite sides of the quilt. Press seams towards the border.

11. Stitch a 14 x 133cm (5½ x 52½in) grey strip to the top and bottom of the quilt. Press seams towards the border.

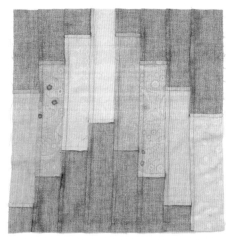

(D)

TO FINISH THE QUILT:

12. Layer the quilt top by placing the backing fabric wrong side up on a clean surface, followed by the wadding (batting) and then the quilt top, centrally placed and right side up. The backing and wadding (batting) are slightly larger than the quilt top. Secure the quilt sandwich by tacking (basting) or with quilters' pins placed at regular intervals.

13. The quilt is machine quilted with a dark grey thread in a horizontal wavy pattern. Start the first line of quilting in the centre of the quilt on one edge and using the walking foot stitch a curved wavy line until you reach the opposite side. Stitch another wavy line from the opposite side of the quilt so that the curves overlap each other in a random pattern. Repeat this from side to side over the quilt, working from the middle outwards.

14. To bind the quilt, trim the excess backing and wadding (batting) level with the quilt top edges. Stitch the grey binding strips together to form one continuous strip. Press seams open to reduce bulk. Fold the strip in half lengthwise, wrong sides together, and press. Match the raw edges of the binding to the raw edges of the quilt and sew in place. Fold the binding over to the back of the quilt and neatly slip stitch in place by hand.

HANDY HINTS:

• When stitching the fabric strips together into the units be careful to maintain an accurate 0.65cm (¼in) seam as it is very easy to let this waver when stitching longer pieces of fabric.

• If you wish to make the quilt larger add another row in a different colourway and adjust the borders as necessary.

• Don't try to make the quilting too exact or even. The randomness of the quilting echoes the sound waves.

Springtime Maze

A simple repeating block creates an intriguing maze.

A simple repeating block creates an intriguing maze.

Size: 133 x 133cm (52½ x 52½in)

SKILL LEVEL: EASY

This quilt is made with just one block design so once you have stitched the first one you just keep going! When the blocks are put together diagonal patterns emerge which, to me, looks just like a maze. The repeating patterns, coupled with the fresh green and pink fabrics, give this project a spring-like feel.

PREPARATION
The quilt is made up of sixteen blocks. Each block, in the finished quilt, measures 30.5cm (12in) square.

MATERIALS

FABRIC
Requirements based on fabrics with a useable width of 107cm (42in):
- 1.5m (60in) cream fabric for the background and border
- 1m (40in) green fabric for the patchwork and binding
- 1m (40in) pink fabric for the patchwork
- 1.4m (55in) square of pale green fabric for the backing

WADDING (BATTING)
- 140cm (55in) square of wadding

HABERDASHERY
- Neutral thread for piecing
- Beige thread for quilting

CUTTING

All cutting instructions include a 0.65cm (¼in) seam allowance.

Cream fabric

- Sixty-four 6.4cm (2½in) squares
- Sixty-four 6.4 × 11.5cm (2½ × 4½in) rectangles
- Thirty-two 6.4 × 16.5cm (2½ × 6½in) rectangles
- Two 6.4 × 123cm (2½ × 48½in) strips for the outer border (join to get the required length)
- Two 6.4 × 133cm (2½ × 52½in) strips for the outer border (join to get the required length)

Green fabric

- Thirty-two 6.4cm (2½in) squares
- Thirty-two 6.4 × 11.5cm (2½ × 4½in) rectangles
- Six 5cm (2in) × WOF strips for binding

Pink fabric

- Thirty-two 6.4cm (2½in) squares
- Thirty-two 6.4 × 11.5cm (2½ × 4½in) rectangles
- Thirty-two 6.4 × 16.5cm (2½ × 6½in) rectangles

STEP BY STEP

TO STITCH THE BLOCKS:

1. Take two pink 6.4cm (2½in) squares and two cream 6.4cm (2½in) squares and stitch together to make two units. Press seams towards the pink fabric.

2. Take the two units completed in step 1 and, keeping the pink square on the left, stitch a cream 6.4 × 11.5cm (2½ × 4½in) rectangle to the top. Press seams towards the pink square **(A)**.

3. Take the two units completed in step 2 and stitch a pink 6.4 × 11.5cm (2½ × 4½in) rectangle to the right-hand side. Press seams towards the pink rectangle **(B)**.

4. Take the two units completed in step 3 and stitch a pink 6.4 × 16.5cm (2½ × 6½in) rectangle to the top. Press seams towards the pink rectangle. Put these units to one side **(C)**.

5. Take two green 6.4cm (2½in) squares and two cream 6.4cm (2½in) squares and stitch together to make two units. Press seams towards the green fabric.

(A)

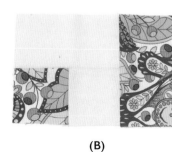

(B)

(C)

(D)

6. Take the two units completed in step 5 and keeping the green square on the left, stitch a green 6.4 x 11.5cm (2½ x 4½in) rectangle to the top. Press seams towards the green square **(D)**.

7. Take the two units completed in step 6 and stitch a cream 6.4 x 11.5cm (2½ x 4½in) rectangle to the left-hand side. Press seams towards the green rectangle **(E)**.

8. Take the two units completed in step 7 and stitch a cream 6.4 x 16.5cm (2½ x 6½in) rectangle to the top. Press seams towards the green rectangle **(F)**.

9. Take the two pink units completed in step 4 and stitch each to a green unit completed in step 8 to make two rows. Press seams towards the pink fabric and stitch the rows together, matching the seams. Press seam downwards **(G)**.

10. Continue in this way, making sixteen blocks in total. For eight of the blocks press the final centre seam downwards, and for the remaining eight blocks press the final centre seam upwards.

TO STITCH THE BLOCKS TOGETHER:

11. Lay out the sixteen blocks in a grid design four across and four down, alternating the blocks with the centre seam pressed upwards or downwards.

12. Stitch together the blocks in horizontal rows. Press the seams in each row in opposite directions.

13. Stitch the rows together. Press all seams downwards.

TO STITCH THE OUTER BORDER:

14. Stitch a 6.4 x 123cm (2½ x 48½in) cream strip to each side of the quilt. Press seams towards the border.

15. Stitch a 6.4 x 133cm (2½ x 52½in) cream strip to the top and bottom of the quilt. Press seams towards the border.

(E)

(F)

(G)

TO FINISH THE QUILT:

16. Layer the quilt top by placing the backing fabric wrong side up on a clean surface, followed by the wadding (batting) and then the quilt top, centrally placed and right side up. The backing and wadding (batting) are slightly larger than the quilt top. Secure the quilt sandwich by tacking (basting) or with quilters' pins placed at regular intervals.

17. The quilt is machine quilted with a beige thread in diagonal lines through the centre of each block and then in lines approximately 10cm (4in) apart. The diagonal lines are then repeated in the opposite direction to achieve a cross hatch type pattern

18. To bind the quilt, trim the excess backing and wadding (batting) level with the quilt top edges. Stitch the green binding strips together to form one continuous strip. Press seams open to reduce bulk. Fold the strip in half lengthwise, wrong sides together, and press. Match the raw edges of the binding to the raw edges of the quilt and sew in place. Fold the binding over to the back of the quilt and neatly slip stitch in place by hand.

HANDY HINTS:

• I have kept the fabric choice really simple in this quilt by just using two different fabrics. However, you could make another block using two different fabrics and alternate the layout, creating a very striking effect.

• There is more pink fabric in the quilt than green, and so I used the green for the binding to balance out the colours across the quilt.

Squares in the Corner

A vibrant quilt of many squares.

A vibrant quilt of many squares.

Size: 140 x 171cm (55 x 67½in)

SKILL LEVEL: REQUIRES EXPERIENCE

This cleverly constructed quilt showcases the bright pink, grey, turquoise and lime fabric choices. The small darker squares and thin inner border help to accentuate the crisp colours of this project, while the white background fabric keeps the quilt light and bright.

PREPARATION
The quilt is made up of twelve blocks. Each block, in the finished quilt, measures 31.75cm (12½in) square. Additional part blocks are added to the outer border to continue the design.

MATERIALS

FABRIC
Requirements based on fabrics with a useable width of 107cm (42in):
- 1.75m (70in) white fabric for the background
- 75cm (30in) each of pink, grey, turquoise and lime fabrics for the large squares and binding
- 50cm (20in) brown fabric for the small squares, inner border and binding
- 152 x 183cm (60 x 72in) lime fabric for the backing

WADDING (BATTING)
- 152 x 183cm (60 x 72in)

HABERDASHERY
- Neutral thread for piecing
- Beige thread for quilting

CUTTING

All cutting instructions include a 0.65cm (¼in) seam allowance.

White fabric
- Forty-eight 7.5 x 14cm (3 x 5½in) rectangles
- Forty-eight 7.5cm (3in) squares
- Fourteen 7.5 x 14cm (3 x 5½in) rectangles for the outer border
- Thirty-two 7.5cm (3in) squares
- Ten 7.5 x 26.5cm (3 x 10½in) rectangles for the outer border
- Eight 7.5 x 29cm (3 x 11½in) rectangles for the outer border

Pink fabric and grey fabric
- Twelve 7.5 x 14cm (3 x 5½in) rectangles
- Twelve 7.5cm (3in) squares for the outer border
- Twelve 7.5 x 14cm (3 x 5½in) rectangles for the outer border
- Twelve 7.5cm (3in) squares

Turquoise fabric and lime fabric
- Twelve 7.5 x 14cm (3 x 5½in) rectangles
- Twelve 7.5cm (3in) squares
- Four 7.5 x 14cm (3 x 5½in) rectangles for the outer border
- Four 7.5cm (3in) squares for the outer border

Brown fabric
- Thirty 7.5cm (3in) squares for the blocks and the outer border
- Four 4 x 14cm (1½ x 5½in) strips for the inner border
- Two 4 x 96.5cm (1½ x 38in) strips for the inner border
- Two 4 x 159cm (1½ x 62½in) strips for the inner border (join to get the required length)

Pink, grey, turquoise, lime and brown fabrics
- After you have cut all your pieces cut 5cm (2in) wide strips from the leftover fabric and stitch them together to make a 6.25m (7yd) length for the scrappy binding.

STEP BY STEP

TO STITCH THE BLOCKS:

1. Take four 7.5cm (3in) white squares and one 7.5cm (3in) square of each of the pink, grey, turquoise and lime fabrics. Stitch together in pairs and press seams away from the white fabric **(A)**.

2. Take one 7.5 x 14cm (3 x 5½in) rectangle of each of the pink, grey, turquoise and lime fabrics and, using the image for placement, stitch to the side of the units from step 1, matching the fabrics **(B)**. Press seams towards the rectangles.

3. Take two 7.5 x 14cm (3 x 5½in) white rectangles and one 7.5cm (3in) brown square and stitch a rectangle to each side of the square. Press seams towards the square **(C)**.

4. Stitch a 7.5 x 14cm (3 x 5½in) white rectangle between the grey and pink units, and the lime and turquoise units, ensuring that they are correctly positioned. Press seams away from the white rectangles.

5. Stitch the unit made in step 3 between the units made in step 4, matching the seams. Press seams towards the coloured fabrics **(D)**.

6. Continue in this way to make a total of twelve blocks. Six of the blocks need the seams pressed as described above and the remaining six blocks need the seams pressed in the opposite direction. This will ensure that the seams nest together when the blocks are joined.

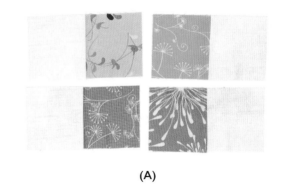

(A)

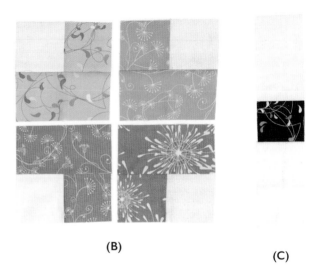

(B)

(C)

(D)

TO STITCH THE BLOCKS TOGETHER:

7. Lay out the twelve blocks in a grid design three across and four down. Alternate them so the seams will nest together when joined, and rotate the blocks in the second and fourth rows so that the colours are placed correctly.

8. Stitch together the blocks in the horizontal rows. Press the seams in each row in opposite directions.

9. Stitch the rows together and press all seams downwards.

TO STITCH THE INNER AND OUTER BORDERS:

10. Stitch a 4 × 96.5cm (1½ × 38in) brown strip to the top and bottom of the quilt. Press seams towards the border.

11. Using the instructions in steps 1 and 2, stitch twelve pink units, twelve grey units, four turquoise units and four green units.

12. To stitch the top outer border, take three grey units and three pink units from step 11 and three 7.5 × 14cm (3 × 5½in) white rectangles. Using the image of the quilt for guidance, stitch them together in a row with the units matching the design of the top row of the quilt. Sew the row to the top of the quilt and press seam towards the brown strip.

13. To stitch the bottom outer border repeat the instructions in step 12, stitching the pieced row to the bottom of the quilt.

14. Stitch a 4 × 159cm (1½ × 62½in) brown strip to opposite sides of the quilt. Press seams towards the border.

15. To stitch a side outer border take three grey units, three pink units, two turquoise units, two green units from step 11, four 7.5 × 14cm (3 × 5½in) white rectangles and two 4 × 14cm (1½ × 5½in) brown strips. Using the image of the quilt for guidance, stitch them together so that the units match the design on one side of the quilt. Sew to one side of the quilt and press seam towards the brown strip.

16. To stitch the second side outer border repeat the instructions in step 15 but stitch to the opposite side of the quilt.

17. To stitch the final outer top border take two 7.5 × 29cm (3 × 11½in) white rectangles, two 7.5 × 26.5cm (3 × 10½in) white rectangles and three 7.5cm (3in) brown squares and stitch together in the following order: 7.5 × 29cm (3 × 11½in) rectangle, square, 7.5 × 26.5cm (3 × 10½in) rectangle, square, 7.5 × 26.5cm (3 × 10½in) rectangle, square, 7.5 × 29cm (3 × 11½in) rectangle. Press seams towards the squares. Stitch to the top of the quilt and press seam away from the centre.

18. To stitch the final outer bottom border repeat the instructions in step 17 but stitch to the bottom of the quilt.

19. To stitch a final outer side border take two 7.5 × 29cm (3 × 11½in) white rectangles, three 7.5 × 26.5cm (3 × 10½in) white rectangles and six 7.5cm (3in) brown squares and stitch together in the following order: square, 7.5 x 29cm (3 x 11½in) rectangle, square, 7.5 x 26.5cm (3 x 10½in) rectangle, square, 7.5 x 26.5cm (3 x 10½in) rectangle, square, 7.5 x 26.5cm (3 x 10½in) rectangle, square, 7.5 x 29cm (3 x 11½in) rectangle, square. Press seams towards the squares. Stitch to one side of the quilt. Press seam away from the centre.

20. To stitch the second side of the final outer border, repeat the instructions in step 19 but stitch to the opposite side of the quilt.

TO FINISH THE QUILT:

21. Layer the quilt top by placing the backing fabric wrong side up on a clean surface, followed by the wadding (batting) and then the quilt top, centrally placed and right side up. The backing and wadding (batting) are slightly larger than the quilt top. Secure the quilt sandwich by tacking (basting) or with quilters' pins placed at regular intervals.

22. The quilt is machine quilted with beige thread in horizontal and vertical lines 1.3cm (½in) away from each seam line.

23. To bind the quilt, trim the excess backing and wadding (batting) level with the quilt top edges. Stitch the binding strips together to form one continuous strip. Press seams open to reduce bulk. Fold the strip in half lengthwise, wrong sides together, and press. Match the raw edges of the binding to the raw edges of the quilt and sew in place. Fold the binding

over to the back of the quilt and neatly slip stitch in place by hand.

HANDY HINTS:

• Leave cutting the binding strips until the very end of the project so that you can see whether a scrappy binding suits your quilt. It may be that you wish to substitute a plain fabric instead of using scraps.

• When quilting the horizontal and vertical rows, start from the centre of the quilt and move outwards.

Starburst

Big and small stars burst all over this quilt.

Big and small stars burst all over this quilt.

Size: 128 x 128cm (50½ x 50½in)

SKILL LEVEL: REQUIRES EXPERIENCE

The patterned fabric in this quilt reminds me of textiles from the 1960s which gives the quilt a retro feel. However, the modern black and white colour scheme brings it right up to date. The small star inside the larger star creates an effective design focus.

PREPARATION
The quilt is made up of nine blocks. Each block, in the finished quilt, measures 35.6cm (14in) square. Five of the blocks have green inner star backgrounds and four have pink.

MATERIALS

FABRIC
Requirements based on fabrics with a useable width of 107cm (42in):
- 1m (40in) white fabric for the background
- 1m (40in) patterned fabric for the small stars and border
- 86cm (34in) black fabric for the large stars and binding
- 25cm (10in) green fabric for the inner star background
- 25cm (10in) pink fabric for the inner star background

- 140cm (55in) square of bright pink fabric for the backing

WADDING (BATTING)
- 140cm (55in) square

HABERDASHERY
- Neutral thread for piecing
- Pale green thread for quilting

CUTTING

All cutting instructions include a 0.65cm (¼in) seam allowance.

White fabric

- Nine 21cm (8¼in) squares, each cross cut twice on the diagonal to yield thirty-six triangles
- Thirty-six 10cm (4in) squares

Patterned fabric

- Nine 10cm (4in) squares
- Seventy-two 5.7cm (2¼in) squares
- Two 11.5 × 108cm (4½ × 42½in) strips for the border
- Two 11.5 × 128cm (4½ × 50½in) strips for the border (join to get the required length)

Black fabric

- Thirty-six 11cm (4⅜in) squares, each cross once cut on the diagonal to yield seventy-two triangles
- Five 5cm (2in) × WOF strips for the binding

Green fabric

- Twenty 5.7 × 10cm (2¼ × 4in) rectangles
- Twenty 5.7cm (2¼in) squares

Pink fabric

- Sixteen 5.7 × 10cm (2¼ × 4in) rectangles
- Sixteen 5.7cm (2¼in) squares

STEP BY STEP

TO STITCH THE BLOCKS:

1. Take eight 5.7cm (2¼in) patterned squares and draw a line on the diagonal from corner to corner on the wrong side of each square.

2. Take four 5.7 × 10cm (2¼ × 4in) green rectangles and place a patterned square on one end of each rectangle. Stitch on the drawn diagonal line. Trim the seam 0.65cm (¼in) beyond the stitched line and press towards the patterned fabric. Repeat on the other end of the rectangle, using the remaining squares **(A)**.

3. Stitch two of the units completed in step 2 to each side of a 10cm (4in) patterned square. Press seams towards the centre **(B)**.

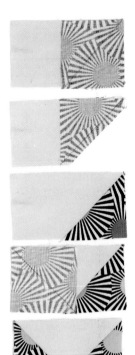

(B)

(A)

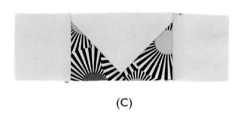

(C)

(D)

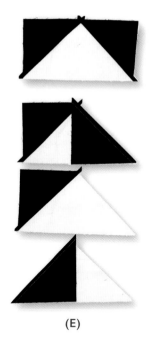

(E)

4. Stitch a 5.7cm (2¼in) green square to each end of the remaining two units completed in step 2 **(C)**. Press seams towards the squares. Stitch these to the top and bottom of the unit completed in step 3, this creates the small star. Press seams towards the centre **(D)**.

5. Take eight black triangles and four white triangles. Stitch a black triangle to one side of each white triangle, press seam towards the black triangle then repeat on the other side **(E)**.

6. Take four white 10cm (4in) squares and sew to each side of two triangle units from step 5.

7. Stitch a triangle unit from step 5 to opposite sides of the small star and press seams away from the centre. Then sew the two rows from step 6 to the top and bottom of the star, pressing seams towards the centre **(F)**.

8. Continue in this way, making five blocks in total.

9. Repeat for another four blocks, but substitute the green fabric for the pink.

TO STITCH THE BLOCKS TOGETHER:
10. Lay out the nine blocks in a grid design three across and three down, alternating the blocks with green and pink backgrounds.

11. Stitch the blocks in horizontal rows together. Press the seams in each row in opposite directions.

12. Stitch the rows together. Press all seams downwards.

TO STITCH THE BORDER:
13. Stitch a 11.5 × 108cm (4½ × 42½in) patterned strip to the top and bottom of the quilt. Press seams towards the border.

(F)

14. Stitch a 11.5 × 128cm (4½ × 50½in) patterned strip to opposite sides of the quilt. Press seams towards the border.

TO FINISH THE QUILT:

15. Layer the quilt top by placing the backing fabric wrong side up on a clean surface, followed by the wadding (batting) and then the quilt top, centrally placed and right side up. The backing and wadding (batting) are slightly larger than the quilt top. Secure the quilt sandwich by tacking (basting) or with quilters' pins placed at regular intervals.

16. The quilt is machine quilted with a pale green thread in vertical lines 1.3 cm (½in) apart. Start the first line of quilting in the centre of the quilt by using the vertical centre seam line as a guide. After this use the width of the walking foot as a guide.

17. To bind the quilt, trim the excess backing and wadding (batting) level with the quilt top edges. Stitch the black binding strips together to form one continuous strip. Press seams open to reduce bulk. Fold the strip in half lengthwise, wrong sides together, and press. Match the raw edges of the binding to the raw edges of the quilt and sew in place. Fold the binding over to the back of the quilt and neatly slip stitch in place by hand.

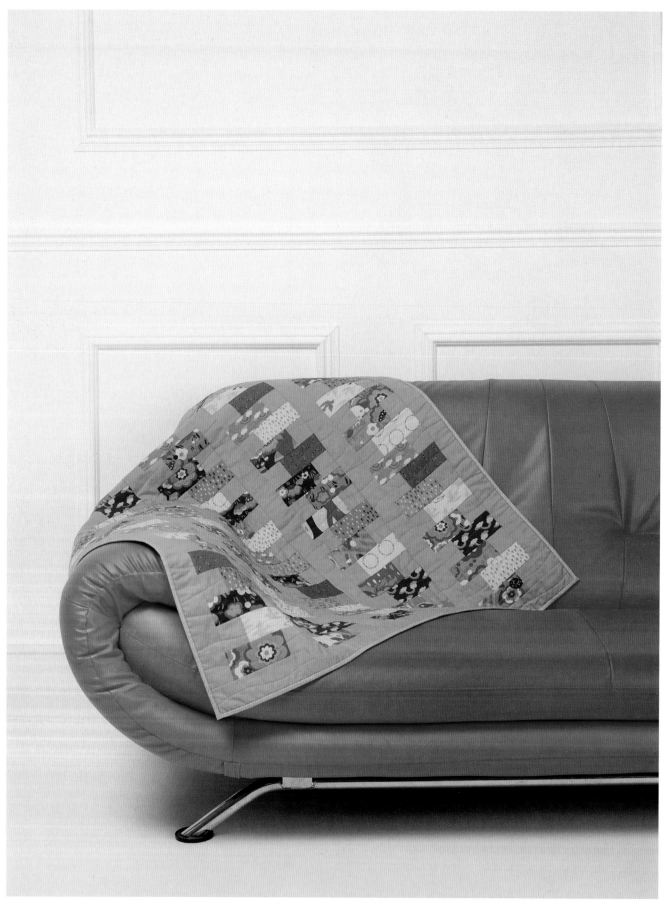

Stepping Stones

Transform scrap fabric into stepping stones with this quick and easy quilt.

Transform scrap fabric into stepping stones with this quick and easy quilt.

Size: 114 x 112cm (45 x 44½in)

SKILL LEVEL: EASY

Sometimes you have a selection of fabrics that just need to be shown off with a simple design. This project does just that, and with clever piecing this quilt grows very quickly.

PREPARATION
The quilt centre is made up of five columns of stepping stones. Each one contains twenty units. If you are using fabric with a directional design, ensure that the units are positioned the right way up before stitching.

MATERIALS

FABRIC
Requirements based on fabrics with a useable width of 107cm (42in):
- 1.25m (50in) teal fabric for the background and borders
- 1m (40in) total of mixed fabrics for the stepping stones
- 30cm (12in) yellow fabric for the binding
- 1.25m (50in) square of red patterned fabric for the backing

WADDING (BATTING)
- 127cm (50in) square

HABERDASHERY
- Neutral thread for piecing
- Dark grey thread for quilting

CUTTING

All cutting instructions include a 0.65cm (¼in) seam allowance.

Teal fabric
- From the fabric length cut two 6.3 x 114cm (2½ x 45in) strips
- From the fabric length cut six 6.3 x 103cm (2½ x 40½in) strips
- One hundred 6.3cm (2½in) squares

Mixed fabrics
- One hundred 6.3 x 12.7cm (2½ x 5in) rectangles

Yellow fabric
- Five 5cm (2in) x WOF strips for the binding

STEP BY STEP

TO STITCH ONE COLUMN:

1. Take twenty mixed fabric rectangles and twenty teal squares **(A)**. Stitch each square to a rectangle **(B)**. Press seams towards the teal squares.

2. Stitch the units together to make one long strip, reversing every second unit so that an alternating pattern emerges. Make sure that the long strip begins with the teal square in the top left-hand corner **(C)**. Press all seams downwards **(D)**.

3. Repeat steps 1 and 2 to make a total of five columns.

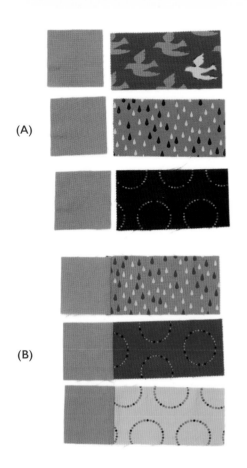

(A)

(B)

(C)

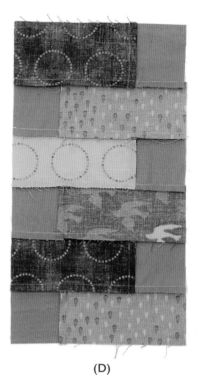

(D)

TO STITCH THE COLUMNS TOGETHER:

4. Stitch a 6.3 x 103cm (2½ x 40½in) strip of teal fabric to the left-hand side of each column. When you get to the last column, stitch the last teal strip to the right-hand side so it has a strip sewn to both sides.

5. Stitch the columns together, alternating the end that you start sewing so that the rows stay straight and the quilt does not distort. Press seams towards the teal strips.

6. Stitch the 6.3 x 114cm (2½ x 45in) strips of teal fabric to the top and bottom of the quilt. Press seams towards the teal strips.

TO FINISH THE QUILT:

7. Layer the quilt top by placing the backing fabric wrong side up on a clean surface, followed by the wadding (batting) and then the quilt top, centrally placed and right side up. The backing and wadding are slightly larger than the quilt top. Secure the quilt sandwich by tacking (basting) or with quilters' pins placed at regular intervals.

8. The quilt is machine quilted with a dark grey thread in a horizontal wavy pattern. Start the first line of quilting in the centre of the quilt on one edge and, using the walking foot, stitch a wavy line through one horizontal line of stepping stones until you reach the opposite side. Repeat this through each horizontal line of stepping stones, working from the middle outwards.

9. To bind the quilt, trim the excess backing and wadding (batting) level with the quilt top edges. Stitch the yellow binding strips together to form one continuous strip. Press seams open to reduce bulk. Fold the strip in half lengthwise, wrong sides together, and press. Match the raw edges of the binding to the raw edges of the quilt and sew in place. Fold the binding over to the back of the quilt and neatly slip stitch in place by hand.

HANDY HINTS:

• When cutting the teal strips you may wish to add an additional small amount of fabric to the length of each strip. This allows you to adjust the measurement later when stitching the strip to the stepping stones in case your seam allowances are slightly smaller or larger than 0.65cm (¼in).

• This project can be made using packs of pre-cut fabrics. For example, if you were to use pre-cut 12.7cm (5in) squares you would need to cut these in half to yield two rectangles from each square. If you were to use 25cm (10in) pre-cut squares you would be able to cut eight rectangles from each square.

• If you are using fabrics that have a directional print it can help to lay the rectangles out first into the columns before stitching to ensure that the fabrics are correctly orientated.

Scrap Happy

Use fabric scraps to stitch a sunshine quilt of flower blocks.

Use fabric scraps to stitch a sunshine quilt of flower blocks.

Size: 98 x 128cm (38½ x 50½in)

SKILL LEVEL: EASY

A fresh, sunny quilt to brighten your day. This project could be made using fabric scraps or alternatively constructed from a co-ordinated fabric range. The single repeated block with its pale grey fabric background gives the quilt a warm and sunny feel.

PREPARATION

The quilt is made up of twelve blocks. Each block, in the finished quilt, measures 25.4cm (10in) square. Sashing strips are stitched between each block.

MATERIALS

FABRIC
Requirements based on fabrics with a useable width of 107cm (42in):
- 1.3m (51in) pale grey fabric for the background, sashing and outer border
- Twelve 15.2cm (6in) different brightly coloured fabrics for the patchwork and binding
- 107 x 137cm (42 x 54in) yellow patterned fabric for the backing

WADDING (BATTING)
- 107 x 137cm (42 x 54in)

HABERDASHERY
- Neutral thread for piecing
- Pale grey thread for quilting

CUTTING

All cutting instructions include a 0.65cm (¼in) seam allowance.

Pale grey fabric

- Ninety-six 6.3cm (2½in) squares
- Forty-eight 4 × 12.7cm (1½ × 5in) strips
- Eight 6.3 × 26.7cm (2½ × 10½in) strips for the sashing
- Five 6.3 × 87.6cm (2½ × 34½in) strips for the sashing and outer border
- Two 6.3 × 128cm (2½ × 50½in) strips for the outer border (join to get the required length)

Brightly coloured fabrics

- From each of the twelve fabrics cut:
- Four 12.7cm (5in) squares
- One 4cm (1½in) square
- From the leftover fabrics, after you have cut all the pieces, cut and stitch together several 5cm (2in) wide strips totalling 4½m (180in) in length for the scrappy binding.

STEP BY STEP

TO STITCH THE BLOCKS:

1. To make one block, take eight 6.3cm (2½in) grey squares and draw a line on the diagonal from corner to corner on the wrong side of each square.

2. Take four 12.7cm (5in) squares of one of the brightly coloured fabrics and on each one place a grey square in one corner **(A)**. Stitch along the drawn line. Trim the seam 0.65cm (¼in) beyond the stitched line, flip back the triangle and press the seams towards the brightly coloured fabric. Repeat on the opposite corners **(B)**.

3. Take four 4 × 12.7cm (1½ × 5in) grey strips, a 4cm (1½in) brightly coloured fabric square, and the four units from step 2. Lay them out on a surface **(C)**. Stitch the units completed in step 2 to each side of a strip and press seams towards the strips.

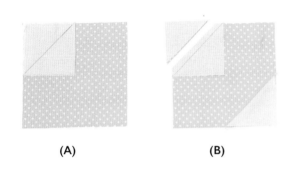

(A)　　　　　(B)

(C)

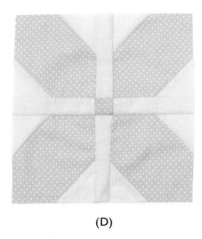

(D)

4. Stitch a 4 × 12.7cm (1½ × 5in) grey strip to each side of the 4cm (1½in) coloured fabric square. Press seams towards the strips.

5. Stitch the units completed in step 3 to each side of the unit completed in step 4. Press seams towards the centre **(D)**.

6. Continue in this way, making a total of twelve blocks with each one from a different brightly coloured fabric.

TO STITCH THE BLOCKS TOGETHER:

7. Lay out the twelve blocks in a grid design three across and four down, ensuring that the colours are evenly distributed across the quilt.

8. Stitch a 6.3 × 26.7cm (2½ × 10½in) grey sashing strip between each block to create four rows. Press seams towards the sashing strip.

9. Stitch a 6.3 × 87.6cm (2½ × 34½in) grey sashing strip between each row. Press seams towards the sashing strip.

TO STITCH THE OUTER BORDER:

10. Stitch a 6.3 × 87.6cm (2½ × 34½in) grey strip to the top and bottom of the quilt. Press seams away from the centre of the quilt.

11. Stitch a 6.3 × 128cm (2½ × 50½in) grey strip to opposite sides of the quilt. Press seams away from the centre of the quilt.

TO FINISH THE QUILT:

12. Layer the quilt top by placing the backing fabric wrong side up on a clean surface, followed by the wadding (batting) and then the quilt top, centrally placed and right side up. The backing and wadding (batting) are slightly larger than the quilt top. Secure the quilt sandwich by tacking (basting) or with quilters' pins placed at regular intervals.

13. The quilt is machine quilted with pale grey thread in vertical lines 1.3cm (½in) apart. Start the first line of quilting in the centre of the quilt by using the vertical centre seam line as a guide. After this, use the width of the walking foot as a guide.

14. To bind the quilt, trim the excess backing and wadding (batting) level with the quilt top edges. Stitch the binding strips together to form one continuous strip. Press seams open to reduce bulk. Fold the strip in half lengthwise, wrong sides together, and press. Match the raw edges of the binding to the raw edges of the quilt and sew in place. Fold the binding over to the back of the quilt and neatly slip stitch in place by hand.

HANDY HINTS:

• It is possible to use fabrics with a directional pattern in this quilt. If you wish to do so, lay out the four 12.7cm (5in) coloured fabric squares in step 2 so that the patterns are correctly orientated and then ensure that when the grey corner triangles are added you keep the squares in the same position each time.

• If you have some fabrics which are deeper in colour than others consider where you position these blocks. I always think that they have greater impact when they are placed in the corners of the quilt.

Techniques

Step-by-step techniques for the beginner.

ROTARY CUTTING

All the fabric pieces for the patterns in this book can be cut using a rotary cutter. If you are new to using a rotary cutter it is worth spending some time practising on scrap fabric, as accuracy does improve with practice.

To cut safely, always hold the cutter firmly in your hand at a 45 degree angle and place your other hand on the ruler. The hand on the ruler needs to be flat with the fingers slightly opened, making sure that your fingers are away from the edges of the ruler. Flip the safety cover off the cutter and place the blade next to the ruler. Starting at the bottom of the fabric, begin to cut away from yourself until you have cut past the end of the fabric **(A)**.

The patchwork shapes in this book consist of squares, rectangles and triangles. All of these can be cut from strips of fabric that have been cut to specific widths.

Before you make your first cut, iron the fabric to remove any wrinkles. Fold the fabric selvedge to selvedge. If you use a 61cm (24in) long ruler you should not need to fold the fabric again but if your ruler is shorter you may need to fold the fabric again so that the fold is on the selvedge. Ensure that all the layers are smooth. Place the ruler firmly on top of the fabric and cut the selvedges from the fabric, tidying up any uneven edges.

To cut strips of fabric from which further shapes can be cut, align the even horizontal edge of the fabric with the first vertical measurement on the cutting board **(B)**.

(A)

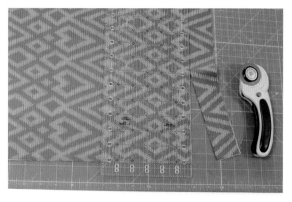

(B)

Close the safety cover on the cutter before putting the cutter down. It is easier to stand and cut rather than sit, and a kitchen work surface is usually at an appropriate height.

Place the ruler on top so that the measurement you wish to cut is in line with the edge of the fabric, for example if you wish to cut a 5cm (2in) strip the 5cm (2in) marking of the ruler will be level with the cut edge of the fabric. Line up the cutter with the ruler and cut away from yourself **(C)**.

(C)

It is then easy to cut the strips into shapes for the patchwork pieces. If you wish to cut squares, place the strip on the cutting board horizontally and then, using the ruler vertically, measure the same width as the strip, keeping a ruler line on the long edge of the strip, ensuring that a right angle is maintained and that you are cross cutting the strip into squares **(D)**. Rectangles can be cut in a similar manner.

(D)

To cut right-angled triangles, cut squares as described above, and then cut the squares in half on the diagonal from corner to corner **(E)**. Make sure that you hold the ruler firmly when cutting on the diagonal as it is easy to wobble and then the triangles will not be consistent in size.

(E)

PATCHWORK TECHNIQUES

The patchwork techniques used in the quilts in this book feature squares, rectangles, right angled triangles or flying geese-style triangles. All of the patchwork is stitched on the sewing machine. Each quilt pattern explains how to stitch the shapes together and has photos to show the stages, but the step-by-step patchwork process is explained in more detail below:

Basic piecing techniques:
Basic piecing involves stitching two shapes together using a standard straight stitch on the machine. The raw edges of the shapes must be aligned precisely in order for the patchwork to be accurate.

When piecing patchwork you do not need to back stitch at the beginning and end of a seam, as often the next seam will cross over it. All seams are 0.65cm (¼in) wide.

If you have a patchwork foot on your sewing machine you can align the edge of the foot with the edge of the fabric to get an accurate seam. If you do not have a 0.65cm (¼in) patchwork foot you can adjust the needle position so that an accurate seam is achieved **(A)**.

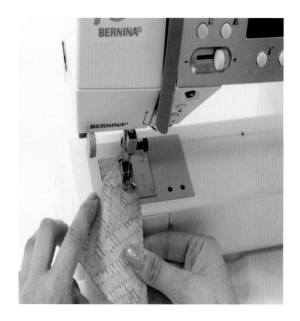

(A)

To chain piece squares and rectangles:
If you have lots of squares or rectangles to stitch together you can chain piece them. Place the first two shapes right sides together, making sure that the edges to be stitched line up. Using the patchwork foot on the machine, line up the edge of the fabric with the edge of the foot.

Stitch along the seam line, but when you reach the end of the fabric leave the needle down, lift the presser foot and slip the next two pieces to be stitched under the foot, leaving a small space between it and the previously stitched shapes.

Continue stitching in this way to make a chain of patchwork shapes. It looks just like patchwork bunting. Once you have stitched the pieces, cut them apart and continue to join the shapes together as needed **(B)**.

(B)

To piece right-angled triangles:

These triangles are often called half-square triangles. They are pieced by starting with squares. To stitch two triangles start with two squares, each in a different fabric. Draw a line on the diagonal, on the wrong side of one of the squares. Place the squares on top of each other with right sides facing and the edges aligned. **(C)**. Stitch 0.65cm (¼in) on each side of the drawn diagonal line. Cut apart on the diagonal line **(D)** and press seams towards the darker fabric **(E and F)**.

To piece flying geese triangles:
Method One
This method of stitching triangles is fast and also avoids having to stitch on a cut bias edge. However, it does waste fabric as you are cutting off and discarding excess fabric. To make one flying geese unit you will need a rectangle and two squares cut to the appropriate measurement. Draw a line on the diagonal on the wrong side of each square. Position a square on one side of the rectangle, right sides facing, so that the drawn diagonal line travels from the bottom corner to the middle of the rectangle **(G)**. Stitch on the drawn line. Trim away the excess fabric 0.65cm (¼in) from the stitching **(H)**. Fold the triangle back and press **(I)**. Repeat on the other side of the rectangle **(J)**.

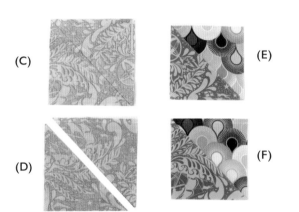

(C)

(E)

(D)

(F)

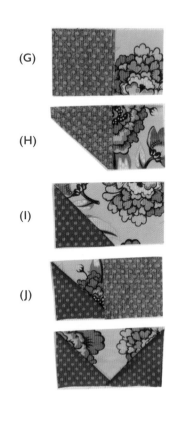

(G)

(H)

(I)

(J)

Method Two

This method starts with one large square in one fabric and four smaller squares in a second fabric. Draw a line on the diagonal on the wrong side of all the small squares. Position two small squares on diagonally opposite corners of the large square, so that the drawn line is running from corner to corner, and stitch 0.65cm (¼in) away from each side of the drawn line **(A)**. Cut along the drawn line **(B)** and press seams towards the small triangles **(C)**. Position the final two squares on the remaining unstitched corners of each unit so that the diagonal line is positioned between the two smaller triangles. Stitch a 0.65cm (¼in) seam away from each side of the drawn line **(D)**. Cut along the drawn line **(E and F)** and press seams towards the small triangles. This produces four flying geese units **(G and H)**.

(C)

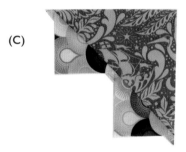

(D)

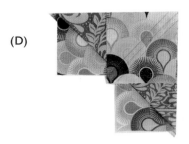

(E)

(F)

(G)

(H)

(A)

(B)

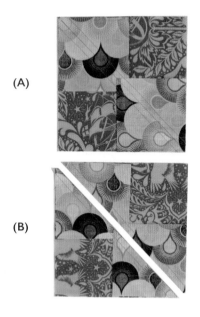

To match intersections:

It is important that seams match and points are sharp when piecing. When seams meet at an intersection make sure that the seam allowances are pressed in opposite directions.

The seam allowances should butt together and can be pinned through the stitching lines to hold the pieces in place before stitching. This same principle can be used when diagonal seams need to meet when stitching triangles to one another. I usually pin the patchwork shapes together by putting the pins in vertically to the stitching line rather than horizontally. The pins can then be removed just before the needle of the machine gets to the pin.

PRESSING

Pressing makes such a difference to the finished product in patchwork. Good pressing ensures that the shapes lay flat and intersecting seam lines remain smooth. To steam or not to steam with the iron? Personal preference here, but I always dry iron and never feel the need to use steam.

It is important to iron fabrics before cutting to make sure that all the wrinkles and creases are removed. If you have stubborn creases, such as the line in the centre of fabric where it has been folded around a bolt, spray

starch can help eliminate this mark. All the seams in the quilt patterns in this book are pressed to one side. The only exception is if there is a very bulky seam, and where this occurs the seams are pressed open. As you complete each stage of patchwork it is important to press the seams before moving on to the next step or adding another shape or fabric strip. Each pattern details which direction to press the seams so that in further steps the pieces will butt together.

Where possible, try to press seams in one direction from the right side of the fabric towards the darker fabric. This helps to make sure that there are no little creases or folds in the seam line. Gently press the seams rather than using a backwards and forwards motion with the iron.

PREPARATION FOR QUILTING

Once you have finished your patchwork top, you need your wadding (batting), and backing fabric. All the measurements in the patterns for the backing and wadding (batting) are at least 10cm (4in) larger than the quilt top to allow for movement when quilting. You will also need some quilters' safety pins. These come in different sizes, and you can buy them straight or curved so try some different types to see which you prefer.

Extra wide backing fabric can be purchased and cut to the required size, however it is just as easy to join two or more fabric pieces to make the backing. If you do this press the joining seams open so that they lay flat. There are a number of different types of wadding (batting) available such as polyester, bamboo or cotton. My favourite is an 80/20 cotton/polyester mix, as I find it drapes well and is easy to machine quilt.

To get your quilt ready for quilting, first press the patchwork top and backing fabric to ensure that there are no creases. On a large flat space, such as a table or the floor, lay out the backing fabric with the wrong side up. Then lay the wadding (batting) on top, smoothing out any wrinkles. Finally, place the patchwork on top in the centre with the right side up. There will be excess backing fabric and wadding (batting) around each side. Smooth the top until it is flat, with no bumps or creases.

Starting in the centre of the quilt, pin the layers together. Work methodically, in a grid format, pinning at 10cm (4in) intervals.

QUILTING

All the quilts in this book have been machine quilted with simple straight or wavy lines. Using a walking foot helps make the quilting easier as the layers are fed through the machine evenly. However, if you do not have a walking foot you can use an ordinary presser foot, but make sure to reduce both the thread tension and foot pressure on the machine to prevent the layers from puckering. It can help to make a sample square of scrap fabric and wadding (batting) to test the settings before starting on your quilt. I use the same thread in the top and bobbin of my machine, and like to use a 40-weight thread in a colour that complements the fabrics in the quilt. This weight of thread is strong, but fine enough to sink into the quilt layers to create texture. Increase the stitch length before you begin; my preference is to a setting of 3mm.

If you wish to quilt in straight vertical lines, use a fabric marking pencil to draw a line from top to bottom down the centre of the quilt. Stitch the first line of quilting on this drawn line then, using the width of the walking foot as a guide, stitch vertical lines moving from the centre out towards the edge. If you wish the quilting lines to be closer together do the first round of quilting, then go back and stitch another line of quilting between these lines.

Each pattern details how I have quilted:

Vertical and horizontal lines
Following the seams in the quilt, use the width of the walking foot to stitch alongside the seam lines up and down, then across the quilt.

Straight lines on the diagonal
Lay blue painters' tape, which is a low-tack masking tape, from corner to corner then stitch next to the line of tape. Make sure you do not stitch on the tape as it makes it difficult to remove. When you have quilted

the first line, peel back the tape and position for the next line and stitch again. Repeat this across the quilt.

Quilt in the ditch

With this method you quilt in the seam lines. As the quilting sinks into the quilt the result is a raised effect without distracting from the patterns created by the patchwork.

Wavy lines

With this method you do not need to mark any lines so it is a quick and liberating way to quilt. To quilt in horizontal wavy lines, place pins at 15.2cm (6in) intervals down each side, making sure your quilting finishes between these lines will help to keep the waves evenly spaced across your quilt. Decide how many lines you are going to quilt within each 15.2cm (6in) marking then stitch across the quilt, from one side to the other, gently moving the quilt as it feeds through the machine to create gradual curves.

BINDING

The final design decision is choosing the fabric for the binding. Using a fabric that is already in the quilt can help pull the colours together, or you can choose a new fabric that complements the quilt. A scrappy binding also works well. As well as being economical it can add interest when there is a lot of solid colour in the border. The quilts in this book have all been bound with a double fold binding. This ensures that the outer edge of the quilt is robust and will withstand wear and tear.

To prepare the quilt for binding trim the excess backing and wadding (batting) level with the edge of the quilt top. It should be square; if not, use a ruler and rotary cutter to square it up. Stitch the binding strips together to form one continuous strip; this can either be on the straight or at a 45-degree angle. Use a 0.65cm (¼in) seam allowance, press seams open to reduce bulk and, if joining them at an angle, trim the ears. Fold the strip in half lengthways, wrong sides together, and press. Starting a third of the way down on one side, match the raw edges of the binding to the raw edge of the quilt and sew in place. When you reach a corner remove the quilt from the machine and fold to create a mitre. Continue in this way, stopping approximately 10cm (4in) before the place where you started. Neaten one raw end of the binding by folding over 1.3cm (½in) of fabric to create a hem, then tuck the other end of the binding inside, trimming away the excess so there is no more than a 5cm (1in) overlap. Pin and continue stitching over the join. Finish the binding by folding it over to the back and hand sewing it in place using a slip stitch.

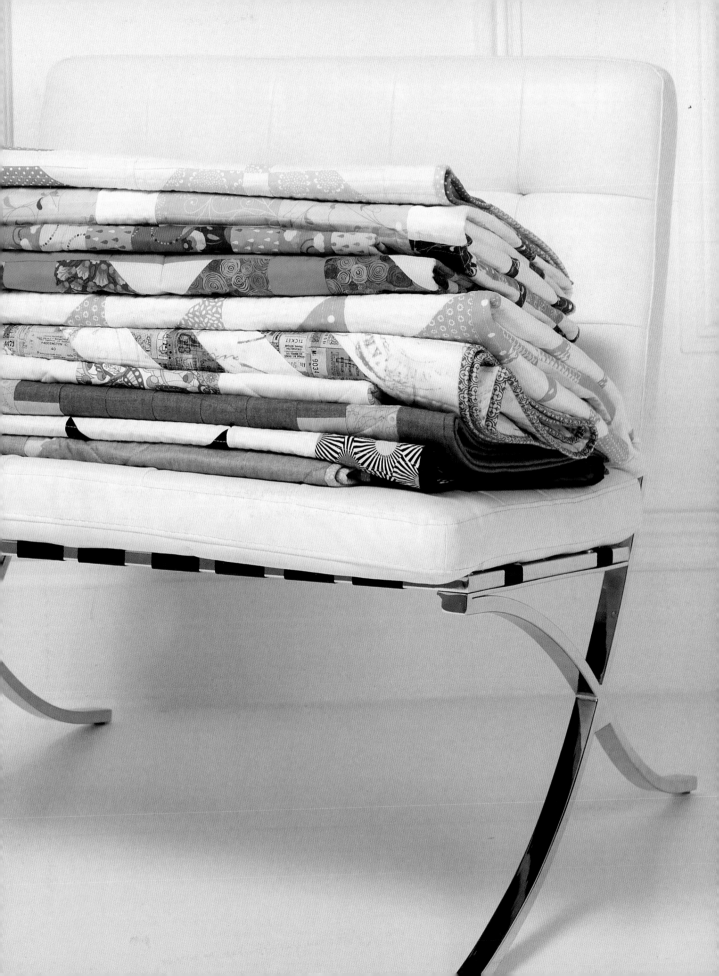

Acknowledgements

I have so enjoyed creating the projects and writing the patterns for the patchwork quilts in this book and am very grateful to everyone who played a part in the process. Many thanks to Darren and Georgina at Quail Studio for their hard work and great design. Thanks to Elizabeth Betts for her technical editing. To Mez Crafts, Makower and The Cotton Patch, thank you for all the lovely fabrics to work with. Finally, thank you to my partner, Alan, who is endlessly patient with me while I talk quilts and lives in a house covered with bits of thread and fabric.

Janet Goddard

SUPPLIERS
Mez Crafts (www.mezcrafts.co.uk)
Makower (www.makoweruk.com)
The Cotton Patch (www.cottonpatch.co.uk)